# WHO'S THERE?

This edition produced for Hasbro UK

KINGFISHER
An imprint of Larousse plc
Elsley House, 24-30 Great Titchfield Street
London W1P 7AD

First published in 1995 by Kingfisher
2 4 6 8 10 9 7 5 3 1

A CIP catalogue record for this book
is available from the British Library

ISBN 1 85697 357 3

Edited by Abigail Willis
Designed by Chris Fraser
Printed in Great Britain

# WHO'S THERE?

## OVER 100 CLASSIC KNOCK KNOCK JOKES

• Illustrated by Tim Archbold •

Kingfisher

**KNOCK KNOCK!**
Who's there?
*Police.*
Police who?
*Police open up the door.*

**KNOCK KNOCK!**
Who's there?
*Isabelle.*
Isabelle who?
*Isabelle necessary on a bicycle?*

**KNOCK KNOCK!**
Who's there?
*Luke.*
Luke who?
*Luke through the keyhole and you'll see.*

**KNOCK KNOCK!**
Who's there?
*Ya.*
Ya who?
*I didn't know you were a cowboy!*

**KNOCK KNOCK!**
Who's there?
*Mr.*
Mr who?
*Missed her at the bus stop.*

**KNOCK KNOCK!**
Who's there?
*Boo!*
Boo who?
*Don't cry, it's only a joke.*

**KNOCK KNOCK!**
Who's there?
*Atch.*
Atch who?
*Sorry, I didn't know you had a cold.*

**KNOCK KNOCK!**
Who's there?
*Micky.*
Micky who?
*Micky is lost so that's why I'm knocking.*

**KNOCK KNOCK!**
Who's there?
*Cereal.*
Cereal who?
*Cereal pleasure to meet you.*

**KNOCK KNOCK!**
Who's there?
*Henrietta.*
Henrietta who?
*Henrietta toadstool but thought it was a mushroom.*

**KNOCK KNOCK!**
Who's there?
*Lettuce.*
Lettuce who?
*Lettuce in and we'll tell you.*

**KNOCK KNOCK!**
Who's there?
*Ivor.*
Ivor who?
*Ivor a good mind not to tell you.*

**KNOCK KNOCK!**
Who's there?
*Alec.*
Alec who?
*Alec my lollipop.*

**KNOCK KNOCK!**
Who's there?
*Egbert.*
Egbert who?
*Egbert no bacon.*

**KNOCK KNOCK!**
Who's there?
*Colin.*
Colin who?
*Colin the doctor, I'm ill.*

**KNOCK KNOCK!**
Who's there?
*Sid.*
Sid who?
*Sid down and*
*have a cup of coffee.*

**KNOCK KNOCK!**
Who's there?
*Teresa.*
Teresa who?
*Teresa green.*

**KNOCK KNOCK!**
Who's there?
*Noah.*
Noah who?
*Noah don't know who you are either.*

**KNOCK KNOCK!**
Who's there?
*Justin.*
Justin who?
*Justin time for the party!*

**KNOCK KNOCK!**
Who's there?
*Banana.*
Banana who?
**KNOCK KNOCK!**
Who's there?
*Banana.*
Banana who?
**KNOCK KNOCK!**
Who's there?
*Orange.*
Orange who?
*Orange you glad I didn't say banana?*

**KNOCK KNOCK!**
Who's there?
*Ken.*
Ken who?
*Ken I come in or do I have
to climb
through the
window?*

**KNOCK KNOCK!**
Who's there?
*Bernadette.*
Bernadette who?
*Bernadette all my dinner and I'm starving!*

*Will you remember me tomorrow?*
Yes
*Will you remember me in a week?*
Yes
*Will you remember me in a month?*
Yes
*Will you remember me in a year?*
Yes
**KNOCK KNOCK!**
Who's there?
*Forgotten me already?*

**KNOCK KNOCK!**
Who's there?
*Major.*
Major who?
*Major answer didn't I?*

**KNOCK KNOCK!**
Who's there?
*Howard.*
Howard who?
*Howard you like to be outside for a change?*

**KNOCK KNOCK!**
Who's there?
*Senior.*
Senior who?
*Senior so nosy, I'm not going to tell you.*

**KNOCK KNOCK!**
Who's there?
*Wilma.*
Wilma who?
*Wilma lunch be ready soon?*

**KNOCK KNOCK!**
Who's there?
*Isaac.*
Isaac who?
*Isaac coming in!*

**KNOCK KNOCK!**
Who's there?
*Alfred.*
Alfred who?
*Alfred the needle if you sew.*

**KNOCK KNOCK!**
Who's there?
*Ammonia.*
Ammonia who?
*Ammonia little kid.*

**KNOCK KNOCK!**
Who's there?
*Amos.*
Amos who?
*Amos-quito bit me.*

**KNOCK KNOCK!**
Who's there?
*Andy.*
Andy who?
*Andy bit me again.*

**KNOCK KNOCK!**
Who's there?
*Anna.*
Anna who?
*Anna-ther mosquito!*

**KNOCK KNOCK!**
Who's there?
*Tennis.*
Tennis who?
*Tennis five plus five.*

**KNOCK KNOCK!**
Who's there?
*Cash.*
Cash who?
*I knew you were nuts.*

**KNOCK KNOCK!**
Who's there?
*Felix.*
Felix who?
*Felix my ice cream, I'll lick his.*

**KNOCK KNOCK!**
Who's there?
*Fletcher.*
Fletcher who?
*Fletcher self go!*

**KNOCK KNOCK!**
Who's there?
*Arthur.*
Arthur who?
*Arthur any more biscuits in the tin?*

**KNOCK KNOCK!**
Who's there?
*Cynthia.*
Cynthia who?
*Cynthia been away, I've missed you.*

**KNOCK KNOCK!**
Who's there?
*Viola.*
Viola who?
*Viola sudden don't you know me?*

**KNOCK KNOCK!**
Who's there?
*Irma.*
Irma who?
*Irma big girl now.*

**KNOCK KNOCK!**
Who's there?
*William.*
William who?
*Williamind your own business.*

**KNOCK KNOCK!**
Who's there?
*Weirdo.*
Weirdo who?
*Weirdo you think you're going?*

**KNOCK KNOCK!**
Who's there?
*Handsome.*
Handsome who?
*Handsome spaghetti through the keyhole and*
*I'll tell you.*

**KNOCK KNOCK!**
Who's there?
*Nana.*
Nana who?
*Nana your business.*

**KNOCK KNOCK!**
Who's there?
*Yvonne.*
Yvonne who?
*Yvonne to be alone!*

**KNOCK KNOCK!**
Who's there?
*Alison.*
Alison who?
*Alison to my radio.*

**KNOCK KNOCK!**
Who's there?
*Scot.*
Scot who?
*Scot nothing to do with you.*

**KNOCK KNOCK!**
Who's there?
*Irish stew.*
Irish stew who?
*Irish stew in the name of the law!*

**KNOCK KNOCK!**
Who's there?
*Lena.*
Lena who?
*Lena little closer and I'll tell you.*

**KNOCK KNOCK!**
Who's there?
*Cows.*
Cows who?
*Cows go moo not who.*

**KNOCK KNOCK!**
Who's there?
*Europe.*
Europe who?
*Europe to no good.*

**KNOCK KNOCK!**
Who's there?
*Myth.*
Myth who?
*Myth you too.*

**KNOCK KNOCK!**
Who's there?
*Rabbit.*
Rabbit who?
*Rabbit up neatly. It's a present.*

**KNOCK KNOCK!**
Who's there?
*A little old lady.*
A little old lady who?
*I didn't know you could yodel.*

**KNOCK KNOCK!**
Who's there?
*Lionel.*
Lionel who?
*Lionel get you nowhere.*

**KNOCK KNOCK!**
Who's there?
*Jester.*
Jester who?
*Jester minute,*
*I'm trying to*
*find my key.*

**KNOCK KNOCK!**
Who's there?
*Snow.*
Snow who?
*Snow use, I've forgotten my key again.*

**KNOCK KNOCK!**
Who's there?
*Adelia.*
Adelia who?
*Adelia the cards and we'll play poker.*

**KNOCK KNOCK!**
Who's there?
*Eva.*
Eva who?
*Eva you're deaf or your doorbell isn't working.*

**KNOCK KNOCK!**
Who's there?
*Phyllis.*
Phyllis who?
*Phyllis in on the news.*

**KNOCK KNOCK!**

Who's there?

*Oscar.*

Oscar who?

*Oscar silly question, get a silly answer.*

**KNOCK KNOCK!**

Who's there?

*Francis.*

Francis who?

*Francis on the other side of the Channel.*

**KNOCK KNOCK!**
Who's there?
*Dimitri.*
Dimitri who?
*Dimitri is where lamb chops grow.*

**KNOCK KNOCK!**
Who's there?
*Scold.*
Scold who?
*Scold outside.*

**KNOCK KNOCK!**
Who's there?
*Jamaica.*
Jamaica who?
*Jamaica mistake?*

**KNOCK KNOCK!**
Who's there?
*Leaf.*
Leaf who?
*Leaf me alone!*

**KNOCK KNOCK!**
Who's there?
*Turnip.*
Turnip who?
*Turnip the heat,*
*it's cold in here.*

**KNOCK KNOCK!**
Who's there?
*Warrior.*
Warrior who?
*Warrior been all my life?*

**KNOCK KNOCK!**
Who's there?
*Midas.*
Midas who?
*Midas well open the door.*

**KNOCK KNOCK!**
Who's there?
*Theodore.*
Theodore who?
*Theodore is shut, please open it!*

**KNOCK KNOCK!**
Who's there?
*Olivia.*
Olivia who?
*Olivia but I've lost my key.*

**KNOCK KNOCK!**
Who's there?
*Gladys.*
Gladys who?
*Gladys Saturday, aren't you?*

**KNOCK KNOCK!**
Who's there?
*Robin.*
Robin who?

*Robin your house...*

**KNOCK KNOCK!**
Who's there?
*Stu.*
Stu who?
*Stu late to ask questions.*

**KNOCK KNOCK!**
Who's there?
*Wheelbarrow.*
Wheelbarrow who?
*Wheelbarrow some
money and go to Mexico!*

**KNOCK KNOCK!**
Who's there?
*Miniature.*
Miniature who?
*Miniature open the door, I'll tell you.*

**KNOCK KNOCK!**
Who's there?
*Congo.*
Congo who?
*Congo on meeting like this.*


**KNOCK KNOCK!**
Who's there?
*Jaws.*
Jaws who?
*Jaws truly.*

**KNOCK KNOCK!**
Who's there?
*Pasture.*
Pasture who?
*Pasture bedtime, isn't it?*

**KNOCK KNOCK!**
Who's there?
*Sherwood.*
Sherwood who?
*Sherwood like to come in, please.*

**KNOCK KNOCK!**
Who's there?
*Aardvark.*
Aardvark who?
*Aardvark a hundred miles*
*for just one of your smiles.*

**KNOCK KNOCK!**
Who's there?
*Iguana.*
Iguana who?
*Iguana hold your hand...*

**KNOCK KNOCK!**
Who's there?
*Doris.*
Doris who?
*Doris slammed on my finger. Ouch!*

**KNOCK KNOCK!**
Who's there?
*Sicily.*
Sicily who?
*Sicily question.*

**KNOCK KNOCK!**
Who's there?
*Moose.*
Moose who?
*Moose you be so nosy?*

**KNOCK KNOCK!**
Who's there?
*Gorilla.*
Gorilla who?
*Gorilla me some*
*cheese on toast,*
*please.*

**KNOCK KNOCK!**
Who's there?
*Stopwatch.*
Stopwatch who?
*Stopwatch you're doing right now!*

**KNOCK KNOCK!**
Who's there?
*Doughnut.*
Doughnut who?
*Doughnut open until Christmas.*

**KNOCK KNOCK!**
Who's there?
*Emma.*
Emma who?
*Emma bit cold out here, can you let me in?*

**KNOCK KNOCK!**
Who's there?
*Tyrone.*
Tyrone who?
*Tyrone shoelaces.*

**KNOCK KNOCK!**
Who's there?
*Stan.*
Stan who?
*Stan back or I'll shoot.*

**KNOCK KNOCK!**
Who's there?
*Nuisance.*
Nuisance who?
*What's nuisance yesterday?*

# KNOCK KNOCK!

Who's there?

*Tuna.*

Tuna who?

*Tuna piano and it'll sound better.*

**KNOCK KNOCK!**
Who's there?
*Alli.*
Alli who?
*Alligator, that's who.*

**KNOCK KNOCK!**
Who's there?
*Dawn.*
Dawn who?
*Dawn leave me out here in the cold.*

**KNOCK KNOCK!**
Who's there?
*You.*
You who?
*Did you call?*

**KNOCK KNOCK!**
Who's there?
*Pyjamas.*
Pyjamas who?
*Pyjamas around me and hold me tight.*

**KNOCK KNOCK!**
Who's there?
*Sarah.*
Sarah who?
*Sarah doctor in the house?*

**KNOCK KNOCK!**
Who's there?
*Dishes.*
Dishes who?
*Dishes a very bad joke.*

**KNOCK KNOCK!**
Who's there?
*Oslo.*
Oslo who?
*Oslo down, what's the hurry?*

**KNOCK KNOCK!**
Who's there?
*Watson.*
Watson who?
*Watson television?*

**KNOCK KNOCK!**
Who's there?
*Says.*
Says who?
*Says me, that's who!*

**KNOCK KNOCK!**
Who's there?
*Aladdin.*
Aladdin who?
*Aladdin the street wants a word with you.*

**KNOCK KNOCK!**
Who's there?
*Amy.*
Amy who?
*Amy fraid I've forgotten.*

**KNOCK KNOCK!**
Who's there?
*Eddie.*
Eddie who?
*Eddie body home?*

**KNOCK KNOCK!**
Who's there?
*Beezer.*
Beezer who?
*Beezer black and yellow.*

**KNOCK KNOCK!**
Who's there?
*Heaven.*
Heaven who?
*Heaven seen you for ages.*

**KNOCK KNOCK!**
Who's there?
*Sacha.*
Sacha who?
*Sacha fuss, just because
I knocked at your door...*

**KNOCK KNOCK!**
Who's there?
*Fozzie.*
Fozzie who?
*Fozzie hundredth time, let me in!*

**KNOCK KNOCK!**
Who's there?
*Howie.*
Howie who?
*I'm fine, how are you?*

**KNOCK KNOCK!**
Who's there?
*Shirley.*
Shirley who?
*Shirley you must know me by now.*

**KNOCK KNOCK!**
Who's there?
*Adair.*
Adair who?
*Adair once but now I'm bald.*

**KNOCK KNOCK!**
Who's there?
*Witches.*
Witches who?
*Witches the way to go home?*

**KNOCK KNOCK!**
Who's there?
*Dummy.*
Dummy who?
*Dummy a favour and get lost.*

**This** is your illustrator speaking: it's 3 a.m. and here I am drawing knock knock jokes. I use an old-fashioned dip pen and ink, which scratches and splatters on the paper.

This is Sam, my spaniel. He has just eaten six chocolate biscuits, a box of coloured crayons and two paintbrushes. That's why he's got a peculiar look on his face.

Also, I think he's heard one too many jokes....

Tim.